LIFE IN
STRANGE PLACES

Extremophiles
life in extreme environments

Harry Breidahl

This edition first published in 2002 in the United States of America by Chelsea House Publishers, a subsidiary of Haights Cross Communications.

Chelsea House Publishers
1974 Sproul Road, Suite 400
Broomall, PA 19008-0914

The Chelsea House world wide web address is www.chelseahouse.com

Library of Congress Cataloging-in-Publication Data Applied for.
ISBN 0-7910-6617-7

First published in 2001 by
Macmillan Education Australia Pty Ltd
627 Chapel Street, South Yarra, Australia, 3141

Copyright © Harry Breidahl 2001

Edited by Angelique Campbell-Muir
Text design by Cristina Neri
Cover design by Cristina Neri
Desktop Publishing by Katharine Shade and Cristina Neri
Printed in China

Acknowledgements
The author and the publishers are grateful to the following for permission to reproduce copyright material:

Cover photographs: Cooled lava background, courtesy PhotoDisc; deep-sea angler fish, courtesy Photolibrary.com; hot spring, courtesy G.R. 'Dick' Roberts Photo Library (NZ).

AAP/David J. Phillip, p. 21 (bottom); Auscape/Galen Rowell — Explorer, p. 13 (top); Auscape/Jaime Plaza Van Roon, pp. 7 (top), 10; Auscape/John Kieffer & Peter Arnold, pp. 3, 6; Auscape/Michael Whitehead, p. 13 (bottom); Auscape/Tom Till, p. 26; Auscape/Tsado/NASA — Tom Stack, p. 15 (bottom); Australian Picture Library/Corbis, pp. 7 (bottom), 9 (top), 11 (bottom), 16, 17 (top), 19 (middle right), 22; Dr. D. W. Larson/University of Guelph, p. 12; Eurelios/© B. Malaize/ExtrA PoL, p. 14; G.R. 'Dick' Roberts Photo Library (NZ), pp. 1, 29; Harry Breidahl, pp. 4 (left), 11 (top); Henry Aldrich, University of Florida, pp. 5 (middle right), 17 (bottom); Johnson Space Center/NASA, pp. 5 (bottom), 20 (bottom); NASA/JPL/Caltech, pp. 24 (left), 25; National Oceanic and Atmospheric Administration/Department of Commerce/OAR/National Undersea Research Program (NURP), p. 18; PhotoDisc, p. 28; Photolibrary.com, pp. 5 (top), 19 (top); Photolibrary.com/Eric & David Hosking, pp. 8–9; Photolibrary.com/Paul Chesley, pp. 4–5 (bottom), 9 (bottom right); Photolibrary.com/Robin Smith, p. 7 (middle); Photolibrary.com/Tek Image/SPL, p. 21 (top); Reuters News Picture Service/STR, pp. 24–25; The Picture Source/M. Rohde, pp. 4–5 (top), 15 (top); Thomas D. Brock, p. 27; Woods Hole Oceanographic Institute/© Albert Bradley, p. 23 (bottom); Woods Hole Oceanographic Institute/© Julie Allen, p. 23 (top).

While every care has been taken to trace and acknowledge copyright the publishers tender their apologies for any accidental infringement where copyright has proved untraceable. Where the attempt has been unsuccessful, the publishers welcome information that would redress the situation.

Contents

SEARCHING THE WORLD WIDE WEB

If you have access to the world wide web, you have a gateway to some fascinating information. You can also use the web to see photographs, watch short videos and even search for particular topics. In this book, useful search words appear like this— 🔎 extremophile. Useful books and web sites are also listed on page 30.

Introducing extremophiles

Organisms can survive in all kinds of extreme **environments**:

- in boiling hot water
- in the freezing cold
- under crushing pressure
- in darkness.

Everywhere biologists look they seem to find life.
Organisms that are found in ⚲ extreme environments
are called extremophiles. Many extremophiles are
microscopic organisms, known as microbes. Because
extremophiles are usually small and because
they live in harsh environments, the
study of extremophiles is a new and
challenging science.

HOW DO YOU SAY IT?

extremophile: ek-**streem**-o-file

Deserts are the driest places on Earth. Nevertheless, plant-like lichens are often found on desert rocks and some microbes survive the extreme dryness by living inside rocks (see pages 10–11).

Some of the first organisms found in an extreme environment were the microbes responsible for the brightly colored bands in the boiling water around hot springs (see pages 8–9).

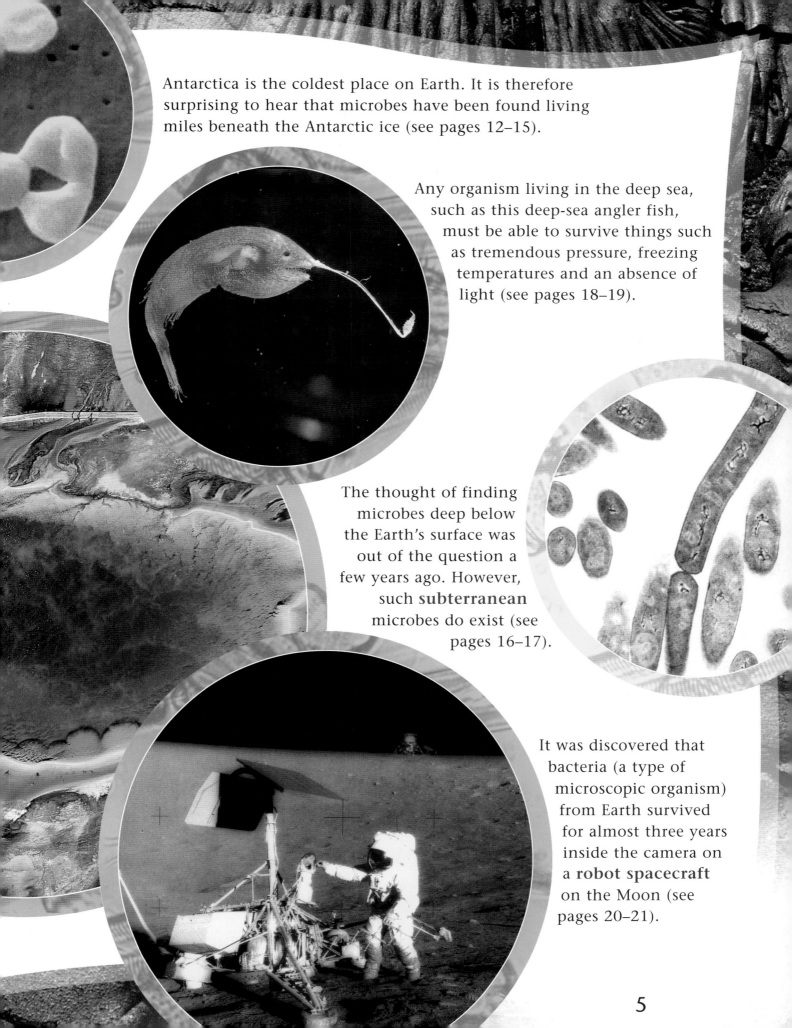

Antarctica is the coldest place on Earth. It is therefore surprising to hear that microbes have been found living miles beneath the Antarctic ice (see pages 12–15).

Any organism living in the deep sea, such as this deep-sea angler fish, must be able to survive things such as tremendous pressure, freezing temperatures and an absence of light (see pages 18–19).

The thought of finding microbes deep below the Earth's surface was out of the question a few years ago. However, such **subterranean** microbes do exist (see pages 16–17).

It was discovered that bacteria (a type of microscopic organism) from Earth survived for almost three years inside the camera on **a robot spacecraft** on the Moon (see pages 20–21).

Background
What is an extreme environment?

An extreme environment is a place that is hostile to life because the conditions are extreme, such as being very hot, very cold or very dry. Conditions in these environments are so extreme that it is hard for most organisms to survive. Although humans cannot survive in extreme environments, we have begun to find ways to explore even the most hostile places on Earth.

There are many places on Earth where extreme environments can be found.

- Extreme heat is found in the boiling water of hot springs.
- Deserts, either hot or cold, are places of extreme dryness.
- Extreme cold is found at both the North and South Poles.
- The deep sea and other places that are totally dark were once thought to rule out life.

These are just some of Earth's extreme environments. All of these environments support life.

Hot springs are found near volcanoes. The boiling water in these hot springs is an example of an extreme environment.

There are cold deserts and there are hot deserts. But it is not just the temperature that makes a desert an extreme environment. It is the lack of rain.

Antarctica is the coldest place on Earth. We know there is a wealth of life around the shores of Antarctica. Now we know there is life in the dry Antarctic valleys, too.

Some extremophiles can survive without sunlight. They live deep below Antarctic ice, underground or in the deepest parts of the sea.

Looking for life in extreme environments
In hot water

Around 30 years ago, Professor Thomas D. Brock began studying the microbes found in hot springs at Yellowstone National Park, in the United States. These were some of the first extremophiles to be studied by a biologist. Professor Brock discovered that these microbes were able to live in temperatures close to the boiling point of water. These bacteria are called **thermophiles** (heat-lovers) and **hyperthermophiles** (extreme-heat-lovers) because they are found in hot water.

🔎 Thermophiles have also been found in other hot springs around the world, and near **hydrothermal vents** deep in the ocean. Some of these thermophiles are bacteria. It was then discovered that other microbes thriving in boiling water belong to a group of bacteria called the **Archaea**. Being able to survive in temperatures as high as 115° Celsius (239° Fahrenheit), these newly discovered 🔎 hyperthermophiles are the high temperature record holders. Some heat-loving Archaea can also live without sunlight.

HOW DO YOU SAY IT?

thermophile: **thurm**-o-file
hyperthermophile: **hi**-per-**thurm**-o-file

The vibrant colors in these hot springs at Yellowstone National Park are produced by a range of microbes that can survive in temperatures close to the boiling point of water.

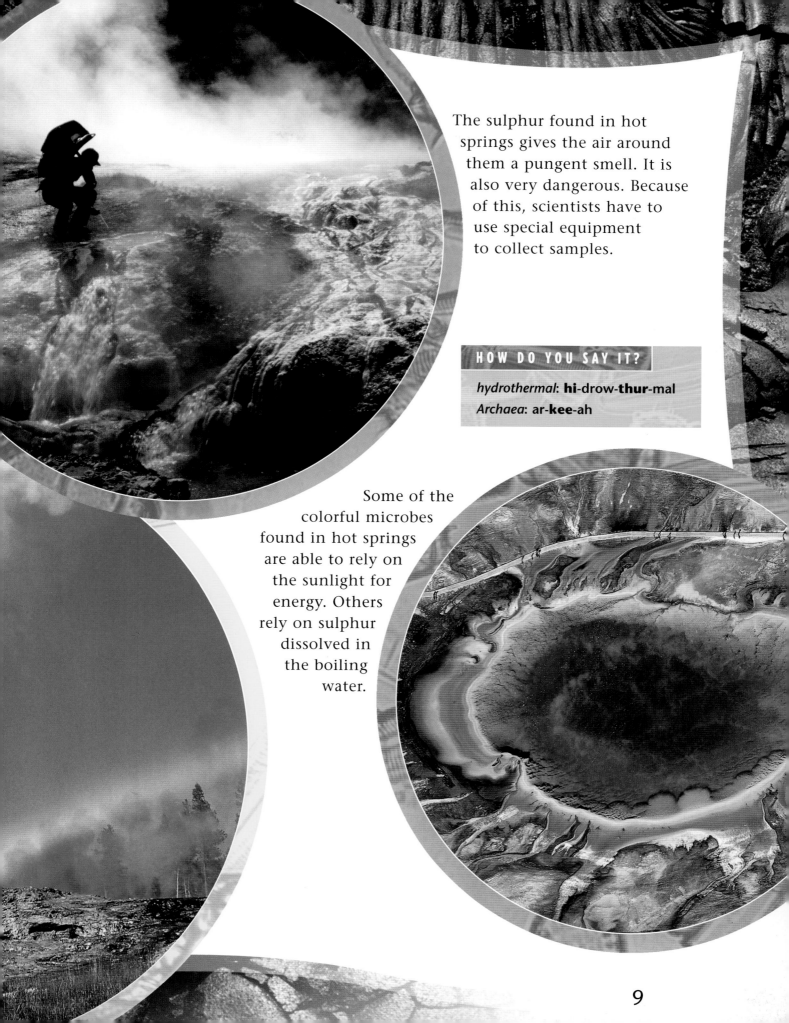

The sulphur found in hot springs gives the air around them a pungent smell. It is also very dangerous. Because of this, scientists have to use special equipment to collect samples.

HOW DO YOU SAY IT?

hydrothermal: **hi**-drow-**thur**-mal
Archaea: ar-**kee**-ah

Some of the colorful microbes found in hot springs are able to rely on the sunlight for energy. Others rely on sulphur dissolved in the boiling water.

9

The driest place on Earth

Also around 30 years ago, Imre Friedmann found microbes (called **xerophiles**, which means dry-lovers) in the Negev Desert, in Israel. The microbes that he found survived inside the desert rocks. They live just below the surface of rocks where they trap enough water to survive. These microbes are called cryptoendoliths. Because they are green, cryptoendoliths give the rocks a green-brown color.

The driest place on Earth is the Atacama Desert in Chile, South America. While the Atacama Desert is actually very cold, it is still extremely dry. In fact, parts of this desert received no rain for 400 years, from 1570 to 1971. In other parts of the Atacama Desert it has never rained. Cryptoendoliths are found in the Atacama Desert. Microbes that live under rocks (called hypolithic algae) and microbes that create a dark coating on rocks also live in the Atacama Desert. This coating is called desert varnish.

The Atacama Desert is home to a range of ✈ xerophiles. Some live inside rocks, while others live under rocks or on the surface of rocks.

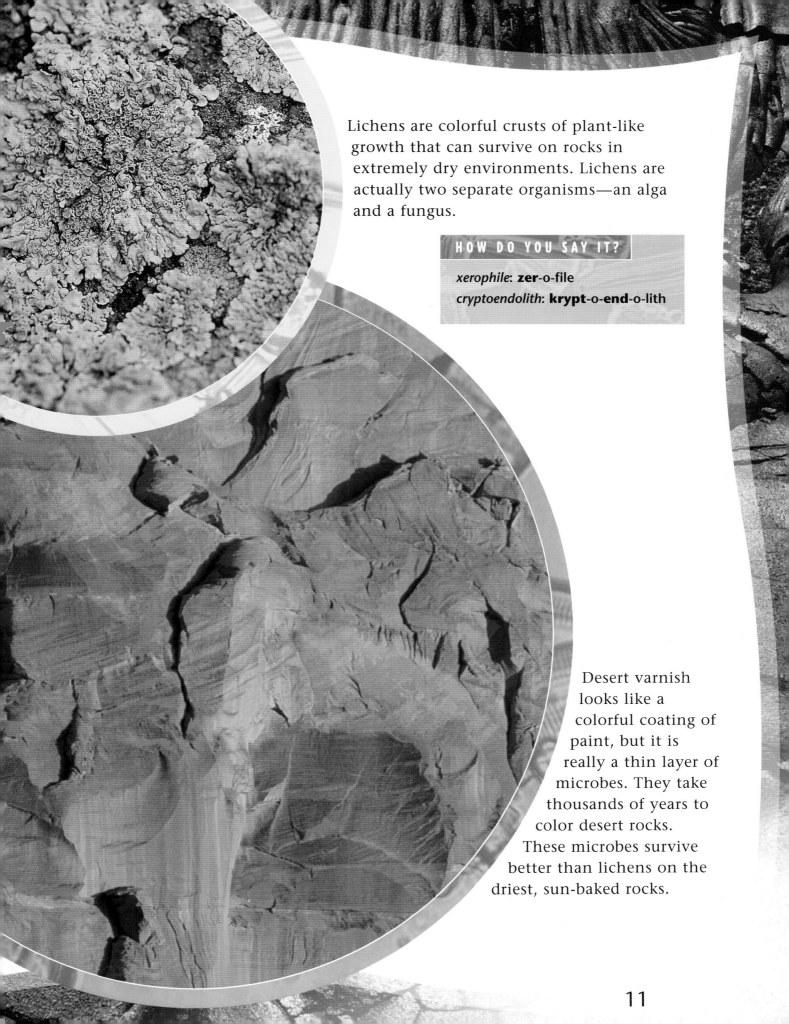

Lichens are colorful crusts of plant-like growth that can survive on rocks in extremely dry environments. Lichens are actually two separate organisms—an alga and a fungus.

HOW DO YOU SAY IT?

xerophile: **zer**-o-file
cryptoendolith: **krypt**-o-**end**-o-lith

Desert varnish looks like a colorful coating of paint, but it is really a thin layer of microbes. They take thousands of years to color desert rocks. These microbes survive better than lichens on the driest, sun-baked rocks.

The coldest place on Earth

Antarctica is the coldest continent on Earth. Temperatures here are often as low as minus 40° (-40°) Celsius (-40° Fahrenheit). It once had a record low temperature of minus 89.9° (-89.9°) Celsius (-127° Fahrenheit). Despite this extreme cold, though, the seas around Antarctica are brimming with life—from tiny shrimp-like krill to massive whales. Penguins, sea-birds and seals also spend time on the Antarctic shores, especially during the brief summer. On land, a few hardy plants and lichen survive.

As well as its snow and ice, Antarctica also has some rocky valleys that are free of snow. These valleys are bitterly cold and ultra-dry. They are home to some remarkable extremophiles called **psychrophiles**. The best known ✷ psychrophiles are cryptoendoliths. They are a plant-like bacteria that live only millimeters below the surface of rocks. For just a few days a year, they receive enough sunlight and warmth to survive. For the rest of the time, the rock protects them from the extreme cold and dryness.

The thin green line just below the surface of this rock was made by microbes. Similar microbes are found inside rocks from dry Antarctic valleys. Some scientists even suggest that similar microbes may have once survived inside rocks on ✷ Mars.

Dry valleys in Antarctica are one of the most extreme environments on Earth. They are more Mars-like than any other environment found on Earth.

HOW DO YOU SAY IT?

psychrophile: sy-**crow**-file

This type of psychrophile lives inside Antarctic and Artic snow and ice. During the brief summer, rapid growth of these microbes may color the snow red, green or yellow.

Under the ice

One thousand kilometers (620 miles) from the South Pole, in Antarctica, is Vostok Station. It holds the record for the world's coldest temperature, which is minus 89.9° (-89.9°) Celsius (-127° Fahrenheit). Almost 4 kilometers (2.4 miles) below the ice of Vostok Station lies Lake Vostok, which was first detected and mapped by radar. Lake Vostok is 224 kilometers (140 miles) long and up to 484 meters (1,600 feet) deep. It is estimated to be between 500,000 and one million years old. Is it possible that life could survive in this lake—so cold and so far below the surface?

Scientists have found microbes living 3.4 kilometers (2 miles) below the ice. They believe there may also be life further down, in the dark and chilly waters of Lake Vostok. They have drilled to within 120 meters (400 feet) of the lake, but had to stop drilling because they did not want to contaminate the lake with microbes from the surface. When they find a way to drill safely into the lake, they will finally learn whether life is able to survive there.

Lake Vostok is almost 4 kilometers (2.4 miles) below Vostok Station. It is not yet known if life can survive in such an extreme environment. This question should be answered when scientists are finally able to drill into this mysterious lake.

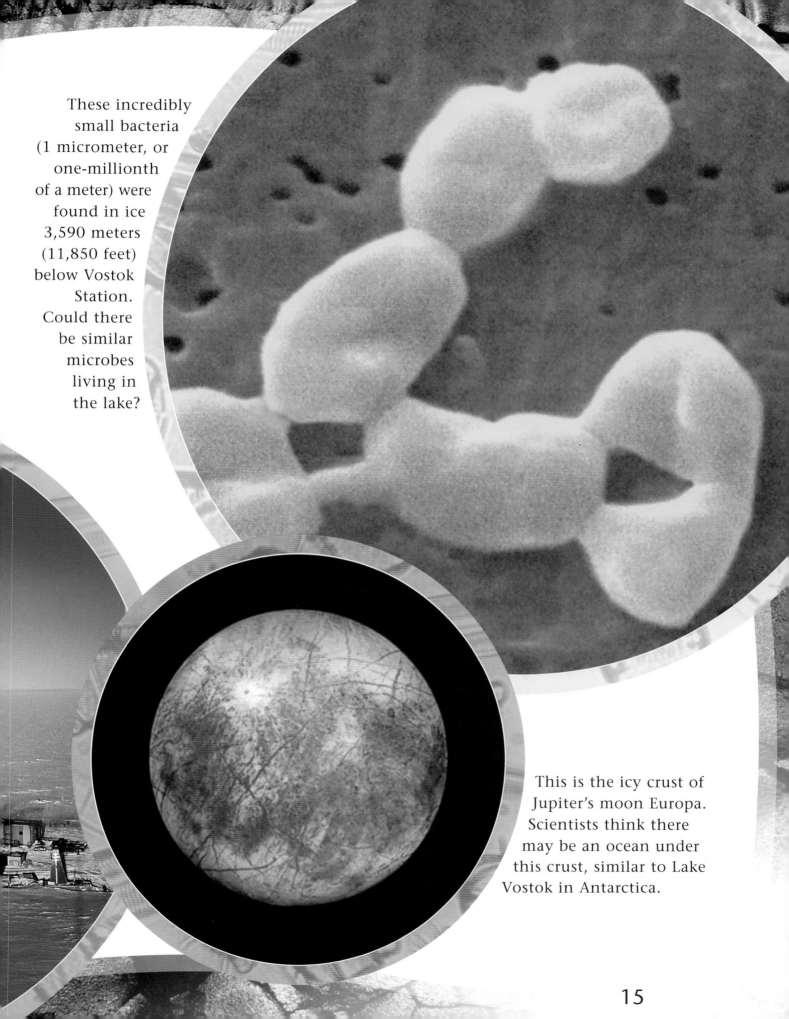

These incredibly small bacteria (1 micrometer, or one-millionth of a meter) were found in ice 3,590 meters (11,850 feet) below Vostok Station. Could there be similar microbes living in the lake?

This is the icy crust of Jupiter's moon Europa. Scientists think there may be an ocean under this crust, similar to Lake Vostok in Antarctica.

Deep within the Earth

Some of the most unlikely extremophiles have been found deep within the Earth. Subterranean microbes have recently been brought to the surface by drilling rigs. In fact, scientists have found so much life in subterranean rocks that they now think there may be as much life underground as there is on the Earth's surface. These microbes survive in conditions that life on the surface would find to be extreme.

Two kinds of subterranean microbes have so far been found. One kind feed on **organic** material that either seeps down from the Earth's surface or was trapped in rocks when they formed. The other kind feed on substances, such as hydrogen, that are found in the rocks. These new microbes have been named **lithotrophs** (stone-eaters). Lithotrophs are very different from the more familiar surface life.

HOW DO YOU SAY IT?

lithotroph: **lith**-o-trof
Bacillus: ba-**sil**-us

Drilling rigs, such as the one shown here, can drill thousands of meters into the Earth and bring uncontaminated rock samples back to the surface.

Rock samples retrieved from deep drills are handled inside plastic tents. This prevents them from being contaminated by microbes from the surface. These tents also prevent the subterranean microbes from being killed by exposure to oxygen.

This microscopic image shows *Bacillus infernus*, which means 'Bacillus from hell'. It is called this because it lives inside rocks more than a kilometer underground, at a temperature of 75° Celsius (167° Fahrenheit), without sunlight and without oxygen.

Deep in the sea

Around 85 percent of the Earth's oceans are more than one kilometer deep. This makes the deep sea the world's largest **habitat**. For a long time, biologists did not have access to this habitat. They assumed it was lifeless because of the great pressure, the absence of sunlight, and a temperature just a few degrees above freezing. Although this extreme environment remains largely unexplored, some life has been found there—at the bottom of the deepest ocean trench, almost 11 kilometers (6.8 miles) below the surface. This trench has been visited by humans only once.

The microbes that live in the deep sea are called ✹ barophiles. Barophiles are a type of extremophile that can live in a high-pressure environment. As well as microscopic barophiles, some larger organisms, such as deep-sea fish and sea stars, also live here. These animals all have special features that allow them to survive in the extreme conditions of the deep sea. No light means plants cannot make their own food to survive, so almost all food must drift down from the sunlit waters above.

HOW DO YOU SAY IT?

barophile: **bar**-o-file

Humans only recently began to venture into the extreme pressure, darkness and chilling cold of the deep sea. From inside submersibles like ✹ *Alvin*, scientists can see for themselves the deep-sea environment, take photographs and bring back samples.

Like all deep-sea fish, this angler fish can survive incredible pressure. It survives in the darkness by being able to produce its own light to attract prey.

In 1977, the crew of the *Alvin* discovered communities of tube worms, clams and other marine life living around hydrothermal vents at the bottom of the ocean. These communities rely on energy from the Earth's interior.

In outer space

On April 20, 1967, a robot spacecraft called ✈ *Surveyor 3* landed on the Moon. It landed at a place called the Ocean of Storms. On board *Surveyor 3* were a television camera and a surface sampler that could dig into the lunar surface. Although no one knew it at the time, some bacteria had found its way into the camera before *Surveyor 3* left Earth.

In November, 1969, a crewed flight was launched to the Moon's Ocean of Storms. Pete Conrad and Alan Bean, the astronauts aboard this flight, landed near *Surveyor 3* and collected the television camera from it. When the camera was returned to Earth, scientists found the bacteria inside the camera. After 31 months in the airless lunar environment, the bacteria were brought back to life by the scientists. This proved that microbes could survive the incredibly harsh environment of outer space.

In 1969, astronaut Pete Conrad landed the ✈ *Apollo 12* on the Moon close to the robot spacecraft *Surveyor 3*. Conrad and Bean then removed *Surveyor 3*'s camera and returned it to Earth.

Many microbes from Earth's extreme environments are hard to grow in a laboratory. The Earth microbes that survived on the Moon were common, though, and it was easy for scientists to grow them in a laboratory.

The microbes that survived for almost three years in space showed astrobiologists (scientists who study life on Earth and beyond) just how resilient life can be. Could life also travel from one planet to another inside **meteorites**, such as in this meteorite from Mars?

Technology

submersibles

The Challenger Deep, of the Marianas Trench (in the western Pacific Ocean, near the Philippines), is the deepest part of the ocean. It has been visited by humans only once. This was in 1960 when Jacques Piccard and Donald Walsh descended to a record depth of 10,911 meters (35,797 feet). They travelled in a submersible called the *Trieste*. Although the *Trieste* is no longer in use, another submersible, called *Alvin*, has been carrying humans as deep as 4,500 meters (14,800 feet) since 1965.

It costs a lot of money to send people to explore the deep sea. Because of this, deep-sea scientists have developed robots to do it instead. There are two kinds of robot vehicles:

- remotely-operated vehicles ✈ (ROVs)
- autonomous underwater vehicles ✈ (AUVs).

ROVs are connected to a surface ship by a long cable called a tether. Scientists inside the surface ship use the tether to control the ROV. This is often difficult, so AUVs are also used to explore the deep sea. AUVs can move about and collect samples without the help of humans.

Alvin can carry three people 4.5 kilometers (2.8 miles) below the sea's surface. It is one of a number of submersibles that scientists now use to explore the deep sea.

Jason is a ROV that can dive as deep as 6,000 meters (19,700 feet). Scientists use *Jason*'s tether to send and receive signals, and to collect information from cameras and other instruments.

ABE *(Autonomous Benthic Explorer)* is an AUV. It is free to follow its own path of deep-sea exploration because it is not tethered to a surface ship. The use of AUVs is relatively new. They will continue to develop and improve in the future.

Robots

Autonomous robots let scientists study extreme environments on Earth. Scientists can also use ✦ autonomous robots to explore space. Although exploration is something that comes naturally to humans, it is a very difficult thing to build into a robot. Firstly, an autonomous robot must be able to find its own way about (navigate) and avoid obstacles. Secondly, it must be able to recognize things that are important, and ignore things that are unimportant. In other words, an autonomous robot must be able to act like a scientist.

Autonomous robots must also be able to return information to scientists. They can do this with television cameras or other instruments, or by collecting samples. These samples could then be returned to the laboratory in some way. The technology for all of this is only just being developed. The first autonomous robots are now being tested in some of Earth's most extreme environments and are being designed for launch into space.

Scientists use extreme environments on Earth to test robot spacecraft. A robot called *FIDO* is being tested in an American desert.

In 1997, this autonomous robot vehicle, called ☆ *Nomad,* travelled approximately 200 kilometers (124 miles) across the cold Atacama Desert. One day, autonomous robots will be able to explore all sorts of extreme environments—on Earth and in outer space.

This robot spacecraft is called ☆ *Mars 2003.* NASA plans to land *Mars 2003* on Mars in January 2004. *Mars 2003* rover should be able to travel much further than previous Mars rovers, such as ☆ *Sojourner.*

Profile of an extreme scientist
Professor Thomas D. Brock

Professor Thomas D. Brock began studying extremophiles in 1964 when he visited Yellowstone National Park, in the United States. He was one of the first people to study this new area of science. He was fascinated by the colorful microbes that flourished in the hot springs at Yellowstone, and he decided to study them in detail. Before Professor Brock's work, **microbiologists** believed that nothing could survive in temperatures above 55^0 Celsius (131^0 Fahrenheit).

Professor Brock was able to culture (grow) microbes that lived in water well above 55^0 Celsius (131^0 Fahrenheit). Since then, he has continued to study heat-loving extremophiles. He has introduced the world to thermophiles and hyperthermophiles. So far, the highest temperature in which these heat-lovers have been found is 115^0 Celsius (239^0 Fahrenheit).

Professor Brock first began his study of thermophiles and hyperthermophiles in hot springs at Yellowstone National Park, in the United States.

Professor Brock and his students have made many incredible discoveries about the microbes that survive in extremely hot water. The work of scientists such as Professor Brock has not only expanded our understanding of life on Earth, it has also led to some new discoveries for medicine.

What extremophiles mean to you
Mighty microbes

The word microbe refers to any organism that is too small to be seen without a microscope. Some of the most common microbes are bacteria. A newly recognized group of bacteria are called the Archaea. Some microbes are so small that 500 of them placed end to end could fit on the period at the end of this sentence. Microbes are the most abundant organisms on Earth, and can live almost anywhere—even the most extreme environments that would kill other forms of life.

Microbes are like miniature chemical factories. They can be used to do many jobs, such as:
- to clean-up pollution and poisons
- to help manufacture drugs and chemicals
- to help produce valuable metals, such as copper and gold.

Bacteria found in extreme environments are of special interest to microbiologists who use microbes for these jobs.

Thermus aquaticus is one example of a valuable microbe from an extreme environment. Once it had been collected, scientists found that *Thermus aquaticus* contained a chemical that could be used in medical research.

Thermus aquaticus was first found in a hot spring at Yellowstone National Park. Hot springs in Iceland, Italy, Japan and New Zealand (shown here) hold similar thermophilic and hyperthermophilic microbes.

Finding out more

Books like this one only give a brief introduction to a subject as broad as extremophiles and the environments in which they live. Some other useful reference books are:

David McNab and James Younger, *The Planets*, BBC Books, 1999
John Waters, *Deep-sea Vents: Living Worlds Without Sun*, Cobblehill Books, 1994
Lynn Margulis and Dorion Sagan, *What is Life?*, Weidenfeld and Nicolson, 1995
Lynn Margulis and Karlene Schwartz, *Five Kingdoms*, W H Freeman and Company, 1988
Michael Gross, *Life on the Edge*, Plenum Trade, 1996

You may also find the following web sites useful:

whyfiles.news.wisc.edu/022critters/index.html
A series of short articles about extremophiles from the Why Files.

www.reston.com/astro/extreme.html
A section of the Astrobiology Web that focuses on life in extreme environments. It has lots of links and a search facility.

www.resa.net/nasa/onearth_extreme.htm and www.resa.net/nasa/otherextreme.htm
Two web sites that give descriptions of various extremophiles and a series of links.

www.bact.wisc.edu/bact303/b1
Life at High Temperatures—a web site by Thomas Brock.

www.ucmp.berkeley.edu/alllife/threedomains.html
A very comprehensive site about life on Earth. Have a look at the section on the Archaea.

www.marine.whoi.edu/ships/ships_vehicles.htm
A web site of the Deep Sea Operations Group at Woods Hole Oceanographic Institute. Go to the sections on *Alvin*, ROVs and AUVs.

photojournal.jpl.nasa.gov
NASA photographs of planets and moons. Take a little time to explore Mars and Europa.

astrobiology.arc.nasa.gov
NASA's astrobiology home page. It does not have a lot of information on extremophiles, but there are a few interesting links and a search facility.

As urls (web site addresses) may change, you may have trouble finding a site listed here. If this happens, you can still use the key words highlighted throughout the book to search for information about a topic.

Glossary

Archaea: A group of bacteria that has recently been discovered. Most are extremophiles. They are also called the Archaebacteria

autonomous robots: Robots that can think and act for themselves

environments: All external conditions and factors, living and non-living, that affect organisms

habitat: The place where a group (community) of different organisms lives under a particular set of environmental conditions

hydrothermal vents: Hot springs that are found in volcanic regions of the ocean floor

hyperthermophiles: Thermophiles that live at 90°C or above

lithotrophs: Microbes that survive within the Earth's crust by feeding on hydrogen that is produced within the rock. Also called autolithotrophs

meteorites: Pieces of rock or metal from outer space that have landed on Earth

microbiologists: Scientists who specialize in studying microbes

organic: A substance produced by a living thing

organisms: Living things

psychrophiles: Extremophiles found in cold environments. Psychrophiles live at 15°C or lower

robot spacecraft: An automatic (uncrewed) vehicle that travels outside the Earth's atmosphere

subterranean: Living below the surface

thermophiles: Extremophiles found in hot environments. Thermophiles live at 50°C or above

xerophiles: Extremophiles that live in a dry environment

Index